The Establishment at Arles

A Play

Barry L. Hillman

Samuel French—London
New York — Sydney — Toronto — Hollywood

Please note our NEW ADDRESS:

Samuel French Ltd
52 Fitzroy Street London W1P 6JR
Tel: 01 - 387 9373

CHARACTERS

Candice Rouget (L'Anglaise)
Mme Tellier
Yvette
Raphaelle
Rosa
Fernande

The action takes place in a first-floor room of a brothel
over a café in the town of Arles

Time—1888

AUTHOR'S NOTE

The events depicted in the play are original, but the characters are taken from the short story *La Maison Tellier* by Guy de Maupassant.

THE ESTABLISHMENT AT ARLES

The CURTAIN *rises in a Black-out. In the darkness, "Grandmère"*
by Béranger is heard (the music for this will be found on page 24)

> "Oh how I miss
> My dimpled arms,
> My well-made legs
> And my vanished charms.
> Once I was beautiful,
> Travelled far,
> But now I'm just a grand-mamma!"

The Lights come up on a room on the first floor of the establish-
ment—a brothel over a café in the French town of Arles. There are
two floor-length windows R, *with their shutters opening on to*
narrow balconies which overlook the rooftops of Arles. The lower-
ing golden sunlight of the late afternoon slants through the shutter
slats. Upstage there is a chair and small table and UL *an opening*
from the stairs draped with looped, velvet curtains. C *is a round*
box-ottoman with a central back-rest and there are two identical
chairs facing each other DL *and* DR. *A chain of coins and a bright*
flounced Spanish dress have been thrown over the chair DL

Candice, an attractive young English woman in her thirties, primly
dressed in a dark suit with a tiny box hat perched over her forehead
in the style of the day—1888, is perched on the edge of the chair DR.
After a few minutes of nervous waiting, Candice rises, crosses to
the dress and inspects it curiously

Mme Tellier, the proprietress of the establishment, enters. She is a
large woman in her fifties, well-proportioned and possessing a
majestic bosom. She has a round face carefully kept white by its
exclusion from the sun—to avoid the prevailing peasant com-
plexion of the district—and intensified by an indoor existence. An
abundant fringe of false black hair lends her a youthful air. Her
voice causes Candice to spin round rather guiltily

Mme Tellier Try it on, my dear. It *is* clean! It belonged to Flora
—my little Balançoire.

Candice "Balançoire"?

Mme Tellier My little See-saw. We called her that because she had a slight limp—(*demonstrating*)—swee-sway, swee-sway! She affected the Spanish look—with a chain of coins round her head that clinked as she swayed. (*She laughs sentimentally*) She left to get married. They often do in this profession, you know. (*She crosses Candice and turns*) But of course, that's why you're here: the vacancy?

Candice Not exactly . . .

Mme Tellier I shall miss her. She and Louise looked after the bar downstairs, but the rest of the girls are up here—(*affectedly*)—in the salon.

Candice (*leaving the dress to follow her*) I came yesterday.

Mme Tellier (*turning*) Oh, my dear, I'm so sorry. We were on holiday. A little . . . excursion, you know. My niece's Confirmation. So affecting . . . (*She sniffs, genteely*)

Candice You *all* went?

Mme Tellier But of course. We are a *family* here. We made a splendid procession, and were the first to cry in the church. It was the prelude to a general hysteria quite unprecedented in the area. A little miracle, the curate called it, a little miracle . . . (*She dies wistfully away. Mundanely*) Of course my brother hoped, by the invitation, to persuade me to make the child my heir—I being childless. But we shall see, we shall see.

Candice (*resolutely*) Mme Tellier . . .

Mme Tellier (*quizzically*) My dear?

Candice You have here a girl by the name of Yvette?

Mme Tellier Indeed yes. She herself is a replacement—a recent acquisition, and fitting in very nicely. (*After a pause*) She is recommending you?

Candice Not exactly . . .

Mme Tellier A very pretty girl.

Candice I wish to see her.

Mme Tellier To see her? (*A thought occurring to her; urbanely*) We do not cater for the Sisters of Sappho here, my dear. Doubtless the staff sometimes form sentimental attachments to which I turn a blind eye, but in the way of business . . .

Candice I have no designs on mam'selle's virtue. On the contrary, I am here to preserve it. I've come to take her away.

Mme Tellier To take her away! What can you be thinking of?

This is a home to the poor creature. Why, here in the salon she
has everything she needs.

Candice (*contemptuously*) Salon! This, Madame, is a brothel.

*There is a pause. Mme Tellier, shocked, and not without genuine
dignity, walks to the box-ottoman before turning to her accuser*

Mme Tellier You are English, are you not?

Candice Yes. I had the misfortune to marry a French hotelier—
much against my family's wishes—who turned out to be nothing more elevated than a waiter when I got here. When he
deserted me—as my family rightly predicted—I was too proud
to return home. But what of it?

Mme Tellier Mme——?

Candice Rouget.

Mme Tellier Mme Rouget. You should be aware by now that
the French lack your British provincialism. We have a peasant
practicality. A *paying* business is a *respectable* business, what-
ever its merchandise. My husband and I inherited this business
from my uncle, and when my partner died—my poor Marcel!
—I continued to maintain the services of an orderly establishment.

Candice You are profiteering from the provision of vice.

Mme Tellier (*severely*) This house is an amenity to the district.
Can you doubt what would become of these girls, were it not
for me? They would be on the streets—diseased, destitute;
disowned by their families—those that possess them. Here they
have security and a certain status——

Candice gives an exclamation of contempt

(*dismissing this*)—yes, status, Madame.

Candice May I, or may I not, have leave to appeal to the girl?

Mme Tellier (*haughtily*) This is not a prison, Mme Rouget. If
Yvette wishes to go with you, she may. Just what do you
intend to offer her?

Candice We were chamber-maids together when we lived at the
hotel in Saintes. I'm sure we could be so again.

Mme Tellier (*sneering*) A fine enticement? A life of drudgery
opposed to the cultural refinements of a reputable establishment.

Candice Cultural refinements?

Mme Tellier This is not a bawdy-house, Madame. Our clients come here for relaxation and conversation away from their domestic cares—not just for their functional requirements! Our tradition is that of the Geisha. Besides, here at Arles, we have a large colony of artists. The district is noted for the clarity of its atmosphere, which is much appreciated by the painting fraternity.

There is laughter, off

Candice (*above it*) Will you at least give Yvette the chance to choose for herself?

Mme Tellier Give it her yourself! I can hear them on the stairs.

Yvette, Raphaelle and Rosa burst into the room. Yvette, in her late twenties, flushed, and with a "Moulin-Rouge" hairstyle, is in a flaming paddy. She carries a painting in her hands and the other girls jostle and tease her, laughing uproariously. Raphaelle is an angular Jewess in her thirties, highly rouged, whose two false front teeth in their pristine whiteness, contrast oddly with the remaining discoloured ones of her own. Rosa, in her thirties, is pretty, but fat and garrulous. The trio dash round the box-ottoman, ignoring Mme Tellier and Candice, snatching the painting from hand to hand

Yvette (*as this is going on*) Oh the pig, the pig—the perfect pig! How dare he treat a lady so! I'll hurl it at his head, so I will!

Raphaelle
Rosa } (*together*) { No, no, you'll hurt him!
(*laughing*) You'll hit someone else. Give it here!

Yvette (*dashing to the window*) A fine pastor, to feed a girl on sermons and daubings! (*She throws the shutter aside*) Look— there he is, still mooning about in the street down there.

Rosa All bones and carroty hair. (*Shouting*) Hi—Ginger!

Yvette (*shouting down too*) Cochon! Move your skinny self—and take your ugly painting with you!

Yvette lifts the canvas high above her head, preparatory to pitching it into the street, the duo squealing and jumping up and down, when she catches sight of the visitor and freezes in mid-air. The others subside, puzzled

Candice!

Candice Yvette.

Mme Tellier (*bustling over to them*) Now what is this brawl about, you girls? Can't you see we have a visitor?

Yvette (*sulkily*) What's *she* doing here?

Mme Tellier She's come to see you, and you will pray be civil, young woman. And what is the occasion for all this fuss?

Yvette (*pointing outside*) It's that crazy painter again—trying to fob me off with one of his efforts instead of honest payment.

Mme Tellier Here, let me see it. (*She takes the painting*)

Rapahaelle It could be valuable one day.

Mme Tellier Ugh. Nonsense, the poor boy hasn't a scrap of talent. (*She hands back the canvas*) I'll go down and remonstrate with him. His friend may be willing to bail him out again. Meanwhile take care of our guest here. She has a proposition for Yvette, and I shouldn't like her to think your unseemly behaviour gives her good reason to suspect she will be successful with it.

Mme Tellier exits

Yvette (*scornfully*) Look at it! The colours all spread on in great chunks, like butter on a loaf.

Raphaelle It's very—*cheerful* though.

Yvette Huh! It's more like a kiddie's paint-box. (*She drops the picture into the waste-paper basket*)

Yvette seems unwilling to acknowledge Candice properly and evades her eyes. Candice, for her part, is disconcerted and awkward

Candice I—I hear you've all just returned from a holiday?

Rosa (*tittering*) Oh yes! It's as Mamma says: "It isn't every day we have a holiday!"

Candice "Mamma"?

Rosa It's what we call Mme Tellier. Oh, it was such a pretty sight, I can tell you: the little ones all in white, and the boys walking with their legs apart so they shouldn't kick mud on to their trousers!

Rosa and Raphaelle laugh together

Yvette (*formally*) This is Rosa.

Raphaelle "Rosa the Jade."

Hysterics

Rosa (*poking her*) And that's Raphaelle. Look at her! Skin and grief. Enough to cut a man in two. Have you come to join us?

Candice (*startled, too quickly*) No! Oh . . . no. My name is Mme Candice Rouget. I'm a friend of Yvette. We worked together in Saintes.

Raphaelle On the streets?

Yvette (*jumping in to spare Candice further embarrassment*) Candy and I worked in a hotel. The only men we knew were the staff there: all hands and no payment.

Rosa and Raphaelle giggle

Candice (*stoutly*) It was an honest living.

Yvette (*shrugging*) Most livings are honest. Here we don't steal, we don't lie, we don't pilfer from our employers or owe rent, and we give value for money.

Rosa (*recognition dawning*) O-hh! She is "L'Anglaise" you are always telling us about!

Candice "L'Anglaise"?

Rosa Oh nothing to your detriment, Madame. Yvette is full of tales of your fortitude and your English civilities. You were her mentor.

Candice (*bitterly*) A fine mentor, if this was to be what I drove her to.

Yvette You didn't drive me here, Candice. I came as to a refuge— after hearing about this place from Louise.

Raphaelle Louise was our wine waitress——

Rosa Till she left to look after her mother at Saintes.

Yvette She recommended the position to me. Can't you see? It meant escape from the slavery—making beds, cleaning rooms, carting hot water—being at the beck and call of women no better than myself; from five a.m. till bed time. You could have come too, I wanted you to, but I knew your English scruples would never allow it.

Candice So you just slipped off like a thief in the night, leaving me a note that your brother was ill.

Yvette You wouldn't have understood. You English make a virtue out of Toil.

Candice You can't *make* a virtue. You either possess it and keep it, or lose it.

Yvette (*walking away*) Pah! You're just like *him*—preaching at me all the time.

Candice Who's him?

Yvette (*flinging a finger in the direction of the window*) Him— Vincent, the artist. Calls me a slut, but he can't seem to do without my company.

Candice walks over to the window, Raphaelle and Rosa following

Rosa He's still down there, pacing up and down like a plucked rooster—all red and nobbly.

Candice (*interested*) He looks—abandoned, lonely. There's something pathetic about him.

Yvette (*sitting*) Huh—he's pathetic all right. Can't paint and can't do the other, that's *his* trouble!

The girls snigger

A mad man. No-one will stay with him more than five minutes. He'd like to get me into that yellow house of his—his "Artists' Haven"—but I'll not go, not I.

Candice Why not? I'd have thought that was your job.

Yvette (*shocked*) It's a familiarity. *I'm* not his doxy; I'm a public servant. Says I'm a fallen woman, but he's a fallen man—yes: used to be the minister at Borinage, but he scared the life out of the parishioners. The funny thing is, he used to live with a prostitute himself. Swears he never touched her, but what do *you* think . . .? (*She winks*)

Candice (*turning from the window*) You talk as if he was—almost a suitor or something . . .

Yvette Rubbish!

Rosa (*bubbling*) Can you imagine it? Perched all night on one of his home-made chairs, being lectured, and never being allowed *near* the bed!

Raphaelle If that Paul was there he'd soon start the ball rolling.

Yvette (*getting up*) He'll not be there long. Who'd live with a maniac?

Raphaelle Perhaps it's Paul he really fancies. A weak man often tries to copy a dashing friend—out of an attraction he doesn't realize.

Rosa Does it by proxy, you mean?

Yvette Rosa! Don't be coarse. Go and fetch some refreshment for our visitor.

Raphaelle and Rosa move towards the doorway

Raphaelle You shall have it on the house, Madame. Mamma will wish it that way.

Rosa And some *petits-fours* as well. I'm starving again! (*Nudging Rosa*) L'Anglaise!

Raphaelle and Rosa exit

Yvette takes the chair and small table from upstage and positions them DL *by the other chair*

Yvette We'll not deny you the civilities, Madame. We're not common at Arles. But—(*meaningfully*)—we mustn't detain you too long. You'll not want to spend the night under this sort of roof—having come to disapprove.

Candice (*hastening to join her friend and sitting at the table*) I haven't come to *disapprove*, Yvette, I've come for *you*. Can't you see where this sort of life leads? Oh it's all very cosy and girls-together *now*, but what is the future supposed to hold?

Yvette (*retorting*) And what is the future supposed to hold in servitude at the *Hôtel de la Gare*, Saintes? Here at least I can be of use and feather my own nest at the same time. What's wrong with that?

Candice (*sighing exaggeratedly*) The French—the French! Their whole history and literature is slanted to assure them that the role of the courtesan is the pinnacle of female professionalism! The men have trained us well: whether we're queens or skivvies we're always their whores.

Yvette (*sitting*) A girl can hold the purse-strings in a place like this.

Candice Tcha! Mme Tellier can, you mean. How much will you have tucked away in an old stocking by the time your looks and health have gone?

Yvette (*stubbornly*) Madame looks after our medication. Did you see those front teeth of Raphaelle's? Real porcelain—and paid for out of Mamma's own pocket. We're the social life of men of quality here.

Candice (*smiling at her presumption*) Oh Yvette . . .!

Yvette (*protesting*) It's true! You should have seen the state they were in whilst we were away at the Confirmation—I've heard. When we got back our menfolk were so relieved they circulated a note to each other saying: "The cargo of fish has arrived back in port. Come at once." So their wives wouldn't understand it. (*Laughing*) Fish!

Candice (*shaking her head sadly*) Local tradesmen, petty burghers —is that your idea of fine company?

Yvette (*belligerantly; stalking away*) At least it's company—I was always ostracized by the staff at Saintes. Here I'm a somebody—a somebody who people miss when I'm gone.

Candice (*quietly*) *I* missed you when you left Saintes. Didn't you think about that? A foreigner—twice left in the lurch in a city of strangers?

Yvette (*contritely; rushing back to her*) Oh Candy—stay here with us. Become one of "la famille".

Candice (*chuckling bitterly*) I'm afraid I haven't your facility for using my body as a commodity. You give it away, as easily as a child giving out sweets, and still retain your emotional control. (*Almost enviously*) I could never do that.

Yvette (*tossing her hair*) Hoity-toity! *I* inspire artists. What do do you ever do? All right, they may never be famous, but I comfort them when they can't sell a painting and I help them spend the money when they do . . .

Candice And throw their efforts in the dustbin when they present them to you! You and your pathetic little boasts. You were always the same—day-dreaming at me, as we lay side-by-side in our tiny attic bedroom . . .

Yvette You don't have to know anything about art to inspire it. I could have been their model. You'd like that. I know you like pictures, I've caught you staring at them on the stairs at the hotel.

Candice (*rising*) Very well. I admit it. I *would* like to be able to be of use and support to a talented man. (*She looks out of the window*) I could easily be fond of someone like your crazy loon down there—a man of sensitivity as well as sensuality. Just look at the poor, tortured creature. (*Softly*) Now the sun's going down, the beams catch his hair and set it alight—a whole skull of little flames . . .

Yvette (*unsympathetically*) Huh! Carrots!

Candice You can see the haunted loneliness in his eyes, even in his great hands that long to hold *something*—if only the likes of you, to assuage it!

Yvette Even Our Blessed Lord loved the prostitutes.

Candice (*spinning round horrified*) Yvette! May God forgive you!

Yvette (*defiantly*) It's true.

Candice Yes, but He implored them to sin no more. Sin no more, Yvette!

A party of women burst into the room: Mme Tellier, Raphaelle, Rosa and a new girl, Fernande, a blonde dancer in her twenties. The girls are singing loudly and lustily. Fernande bears a cake with lighted candles and a flat box, Rosa is carrying plates and little delicacies and Raphaelle has the wine and glasses. They parade the cake to the table as they sing

Rosa ⎤	"Happy birthday to you,
Raphaelle ⎬	Happy birthday to you,
Fernande ⎰	Happy birthday, dear Yvette,
	Happy birthday to you!"

At the song's conclusion they dress the table, laughing and talking, and kissing Yvette, all at the same time

Mme Tellier (*slyly triumphant to Candice*) You observe, Madame, for all your touching concern for your friend's welfare, you had omitted to remember her birthday.

Candice I admit the occasion had slipped my mind, Madame, but I trust Yvette's soul is of more importance than her age. Happy birthday, my dear.

Yvette (*childishly pleased*) Oh thank you—thank you, everyone. (*She kisses Mme Tellier*) Dear Mme Tellier, you are like a mother to me!

Mme Tellier smiles blindingly at Candice who is furious at the woman's guile

And Candy, this is Fernande—the last of us. Blonde and Scandinavian, you'll note. Mamma likes to have an example of each romantic type, so that she can always cater for every man's ideal!

Mme Tellier (*knowingly*) Perhaps there are men who might even fancy une fille Anglaise?

Candice They would fancy in vain, then!

Fernande Oh you mustn't think me the wanton, Madame. This is just a fill-in for me, you know—until I get another engagement.

Rosa Fernande's going to be a famous dancer. She's already had
several parts in the provinces—well, chorus work, really, but
it's all experience . . .

Fernande Yes. Operettas—Offenbach and what-not—but some
day: *Le Moulin Rouge*!

They laugh

Mme Tellier Come along, drink up, everyone. I'm sure, Mme
Rouget, you'll not refuse sufficient for a toast to a friend?

They raise their glasses

All To Yvette!

Candice sits

Yvette Aurgh—I don't think I can take all this excitement! What
with yesterday's excursion, and now this. (*Taking the bottle
round*) Take plenty of booze, everybody. Mme T's paying!

Mme Tellier (*playfully smacking her*) Minx! (*She sits down*)

Yvette (*plumping down beside Candice*) Do you remember how
we spent my *last* birthday, Candice? (*She looks round at them
all for effect*) Clearing turds out of a wardrobe!

Reaction

Yes—turds out of a wardrobe. A count's mistress who once
worked at the hotel as a chamber-maid herself, and was now
back again as a guest and grande dame wanted to impress her
triumph on the rest of us. So she left her own little memento in
the wardrobe to remind us.

Raphaelle (*choking with laughter*) Filthy beast!

Fernande (*drinking heavily*) When I'm famous I'll do the same.
In every wardrobe in France!

Mme Tellier (*in mock horror*) Ladies—for shame! La politesse,
la politesse.

Raphaelle (*nudging Fernande*) Give us the presents, you fool.

Candice "Us"?

Raphaelle Oh yes. It's a case of "one for all and all for one" in
this house!

Yvette (*scornfully to Fernande*) And when were *you* last able to
afford presents, my fine feathered friend?

Fernande We-ell . . .

Fernande sits down and Rosa, Raphaelle and Yvette all cluster expectantly round her

You remember when we were all in the train, going to the Confirmation?

Cries of " Yes, yes", "Go on", etc.

And that horrid commercial traveller man got in and started teasing that basket of ducks . . . ?

Rosa (*gurgling and stuffing her face at the same time*) Oh—it was so funny, Candice. There were these two old peasants and their ducks, you see——

Raphaelle All done up in a basket with their heads poking out——

Rosa And he was pinching them and quacking at them——

Raphaelle And we were tapping his hand and kissing the poor birds——

Rosa And these old peasants never cracked their faces, not once!

Fernande Am I going to be allowed to finish this—this anecdote, or not?

Cries of "Do, do", "Sorry, I'm sure", etc.

We-ell, you remember when he showed us what he was selling?

Yvette (*touching Candice's arm*) You'll never guess, Candy! In a million years.

Candice (*drinking with the rest*) Well, what?

Mme Tellier *Garters*, Madame. As true as I'm standing here. Garters!

Fernande He made us all try them on, till the poor country-couple were quite outraged! And when you all slipped out for refreshment at Rouen, I allowed him a few . . . petites liberties —nothing too unladylike, you'll understand; but enough to prompt him to say he'd never had a journey like it for years—and he left me with a pair of garters for each of us.

Rosa Pressies!

Mme Tellier (*aside to Candice*) You see, Madame—when did someone last give *you* a gift?

Candice Oh it's very subtle of you, Madame, to prey on my feelings of exclusion and greed, but my stockings will stay round my ankles rather than they should be held up at such a price as that!

Fernande (*opening the box*) As it's Yvette's anniversary, she shall have the first choice. Come on now.

Yvette They're all so classy. I'm dazzled. No, these—these, I think. (*She extracts a gaudy satin pair in red*)

Fernande And as L'Anglaise was so remiss as to arrive without a token, she shall put them on for you.

Laughter and applause. Candice rises—a little unsteady from wine too rapidly consumed—and kneels while Yvette flounces up her petticoats and places an elegant foot on the chair. Almost caressingly, she positions the garter. Yvette changes legs, is fitted with the garter's twin, then with her toe playfully pushes Candice away. It is a gesture which reads " You shall not take me from here" and both women acknowledge it. More applause. Raphaelle and Rosa twitter round Fernande

Rosa I want the lilac ones—let go! They'll match my dress.

Raphaelle Pooh! With your great sausage legs you'll never get them any higher than your knees.

Rosa (*punching her and snatching the garters*) Monster! And with your skinny shanks you'll be able to pull them right up to *here*— and they'll still be loose.

She hauls up Raphaelle's skirts and pokes the top of her thigh intimately. Raphaelle shrieks. Limbs and frills all over the place, they pull on the garters

(*To Raphaelle*) You must have the blue ones. They'll go with your varicose veins!

Fernande And I shall take the golden ones—to echo my golden ringlets.

Raphaelle You haven't got any ringlets.

Fernande (*pushing her*) Not on my *head*, ninny . . .!

They howl and chatter

Mme Tellier (*slyly aside to Candice*) Will there be laughter like this when you're back in your hotel garret, Madame?

Candice Don't be cruel.

Mme Tellier refills Candice's glass. The girls jostle into a row with their skirts held high

Fernande Well what do you think, Mamma? Whose look the prettiest?

Mme Tellier (*protesting with a plump hand*) Ar-rgh now, now, mes petites anges. You know I never have favourites. You must leave such contests to the gentlemen.

Rosa Then we could have a competition as to which man gets them off us the quickest!

Squeals

Mme Tellier (*remonstrating*) All right, ladies—that will do. Merriment, yes; coarseness, no.

A peal of laughter is emitted by Candice. They all turn their heads to stare at her

Candice (*gasping*) I'm sorry, but you must excuse my hilarity. It's just that you all look like some grotesque chorus—out of one of Fernande's operettas!

The girls take this as a compliment, ignoring the "grotesque"

Yvette She's right, y'know. We should do a dance now, with Fernande leading—as she's the *expert*!

Fernande
Rosa
Raphaelle }(*together*) Yes, yes!
Yvette

Fernande Of course. The Can-Can. It's got to be the Can-Can!

They hurl themselves into a spirited version of the famous dance, Mesdames Tellier and Rouget clapping out the rhythm. Eventually they collapse, falling in attitudes about the room, and making for the wine as soon as they have the breath to do so

Fernande (*suddenly*) But Mme Tellier hasn't had a pair!

Raphaelle No. Oh—Madame, but you must have some garters as well. It's only fair.

Fernande
Rosa
Raphaelle }(*together*) Yes—come on!
Yvette

Mme Tellier (*protesting but amused*) Oh no, mes chères. I am your employer, not a coquette. It would not be seemly.

Yvette (*drunkenly*) It's *my* party, and I *insist*. You deserve a gift as much as any of us.

Fernande (*in a flattering tone*) You shall retain your dignity,
Madame. The remaining pair are of the utmost propriety.
(*Silkily*) Black, with a single silver . . . metal . . . thread . . .
A nun could wear them.

Mme Tellier (*weakening*) We-ell . . . perhaps just as a memento
of a happy occasion.

"Stately as a galleon" she glides C *and lifts her skirts. A sur-
prisingly shapely leg is unveiled, and with Yvette performing a soft
"drum-roll" accompaniment on the table, Fernande places the
garters in position with as much ceremony as a coronation. "Ahs!"
and polite clapping mark the event as Madame lowers her skirt,
slowly, like the descending of a theatre curtain*

Whenever I wear them I shall think of my pure little niece,
making her alliegances to Mother Church.

Candice (*nauseated*) Tcha!

Rosa (*immediately lachrymose and maudlin, sinking into a chair
and blubbering*) Oh, the dear little mite. She was the babe I
always wanted and never had . . .

Candice (*acid with wine*) I'm sure, mam'selle, you never missed a
chance.

Rosa (*ignoring her*) While you were all asleep at Madame's
brother's—Fernande and Raphaelle in the dining-room,
Madame and her sister-in-law in the bedroom, poor M. Rivet
in the carpenter's workshop, among the wood-shavings, and
Yvette and la Balançoire in the kitchen—*I* was stuffed in a
tiny cupboard at the top of the stairs. It was agony for a lady
of—well—ample proportions, but I forgot my own discom-
forts when I heard the plaintive sobs of a child.

Raphaelle Ahh.

Rosa It was the daughter—used to sleeping with her mummy,
and now frightened to death, having been tucked away in the
attic for the occasion. I called out to her and fetched her to my
tiny cupboard—and crumpled as we were, I hugged and kissed
her till she fell asleep on my naked bosom.

Mme Tellier (*patting Rosa's hair, her eye moist*) You always had
a kind heart, Rosa.

Candice (*unimpressed*) Maudlin fiddlesticks! It was blatant cor-
ruption of a minor. The child should have been ritually
cleansed before being allowed to set foot in a church.

Mme Tellier (*with sincere severity none the less*) Do not belittle
my girls, Madame. When you can offer them something better,
when you can put bread in their mouths—then you can come
again and sneer.

Yvette (*scoffing*) She's feeling out of it because she didn't get a
present.

Fernande But there aren't any garters left. I know—she can have
la Balançoire's dress instead!

Candice (*rising stoutly, though a shade unsteadily*) No! You shall
not make a strumpet out of *me*.

*But she is drunk and the girls too strong. They take off her suit and
dress her in the Spanish costume. Mme Tellier goes to the waste-
paper basket while this is going on, retrieving Vincent's painting*

Fernande She hasn't got a bad figure for a foreigner!

Candice (*struggling*) And you haven't got a bad cheek—for a
Froggie! Leave me alone.

Raphaelle Yes—a handsome chest, and all of it wasted on
waiters and pot-boys at a cheap boarding-house.

Candice The *Hôtel de la Gare* is the finest building in the district,
and a sight less flea-bitten than this den of iniquity.

Mme Tellier Do not tear that costume, Madame. It cost more
than your chamber-maid's wages can aspire to. There. I think
M. Van Gogh's painting ought to sit here for now. (*She places
it against the pillar of the box-ottoman*) After all, it too was a
birthday present, in its own poor way. He meant it kindly.

Yvette (*looking out of the window*) At least he's decided to go
away at last. Did you get satisfaction from M. Gaugin?

Mme Tellier Alas, no. He left today, they tell me—after the
madman had pulled a knife on him.

Yvette (*shivering*) Urgh. And you expect me to take such an
animal to my bosom! I could risk serious injury every time I
meet him.

Candice (*flaring*) Have some pity, Yvette. You must know what
it's like to be rejected and desperate, or you wouldn't have
come *here* in the first place.

Fernande (*surprised and amused*) Oh, they have such fire, these
Spaniards!

*Candice sinks down in her chair and meekly allows Rosa to tie the
string of jangling coins round her forehead. It begins to get dusk*

Raphaelle Give us a little song, Senora!

Fernande Yes. Something sensuous and romantic.

Yvette (*wandering back*) Pfh! All *she* knows is *God Save the Queen* and *Rule Britannia*. What was that song we all sang in the carriage, driving back to the station with M. Rivet?

Rosa Oh yes! That was a good one. I love the old ones, don't you? One of Béranger's ballads. (*She sings*)

> "Oh how I miss
> My dimpled arms,
> My well-made legs
> And my vanished charms.
> Once I was beautiful,
> Travelled far,
> But now I'm just a grand-mamma."

She continues to hum the tune while Fernande recalls the scene

Fernande Do you remember how Mme Tellier gave M. Rivet a slice of her tongue for meddling with you, Rosa? He got all huffy and started drinking and couldn't control the horses, so that our chairs toppled over and we were thrown all over the cart! And the wheels threw up two trails of dust, and we sang till we were hoarse—and all the road-workers stared at us over their shovels and waved their handkerchiefs. We must have looked like an excursion from the asylum!

All, save the scornful Candice, join in the singing

Yvette	"Oh how I regret
Rosa	My dimpled arms,
Fernande	My well-made legs
Raphaelle	And my vanished charms.
Mme Tellier	Cherish your beauty,
	Too soon it's marred
	And you'll become old grand-mammas."

A bell breaks into their reverie, ringing persistently. The girls start up and adjust their clothing

Mme Tellier (*bustling*) Heavens alive! Guests are arriving and we're dreaming away up here. Move yourselves, girls, and clear this mess away. Raphaelle, go and open the door. It's probably M. Vassi.

Raphaelle exits

Yvette, Fernande and Rosa generally start to tidy up the room

(*To Candice*) M. Vassi is a judge with the Tribunal of Commerce, Candice, and an admirer of mine. Strictly platonic, you'll understand, but one day it could be more profitable to leave one's business to a husband than to a niece . . . (*She spins round*) Fernande, close those windows, it's getting dark. Rosa! Light the lamps.

Rosa scampers around, doing as she is bidden, and Fernande goes to the window. The bell stops ringing

Fernande Gracious. There's Vincent back again—all hunched up and carrying a parcel.
Candice (*joining her*) Let me see!
Fernande He's leaving it on the doorstep and scurrying away like an emaciated spider with half its legs pulled off.
Candice Poor brute.
Mme Tellier (*sternly*) Candice—bolt that shutter! And Fernande, go down and see what he's left. I'll take this cake and cut it up for ourselves and our guests. (*She picks up the cake*)

Fernande flies out

Yvette (*shouting after her*) If it's another painting chuck it after him!

Mme Tellier, carrying the cake, and Rosa exit

Candice and Yvette are left facing one another. A pause

Candice (*sobered*) You're going to stay, aren't you?
Yvette (*tossing her head*) Why shouldn't I? I'm wanted here. I'm loved.
Candice You're a commodity—a saleable object.

Yvette turns away

Oh you may sentimentalize it now and wallow in your little outings and sisterly affections, but where will they all be when you're old and diseased?
Yvette (*loudly*) I might as well die of the pox in a whore-house as die of TB in a hotel attic.

Candice We can achieve more than that if we try. Please try *with* me, Yvette.

Yvette (*turning on her*) Is that why you're here, Candice? Just question your own motives a bit more honestly. Did you really come here to reclaim me—save my soul? Or because you couldn't face the loneliness yourself any more? Or because you were just plain fascinated with the life of a tart? Why did you come, and how is it you can't seem to bring yourself to go?

Pause

Mme Tellier, Rosa, Raphaelle and Fernande return en masse, *twittering and jostling. Rosa carries a small parcel*

Rosa He must have known it was your birthday, Yvette. He's sent you a little gift—all wrapped up and bearing your name.

Yvette accepts the parcel while the rest gather round her

Yvette All wrapped up, you say! Look at it: like a kilo of cod from the fish-mongers, and he claims to be an artist! Artistic people do things artistically, this is thrown at you—just like his paintings.

Raphaelle Hurry up and open it. We haven't got all night. M. Philippe has arrived to play the piano and we're going to have a dance.

Mme Tellier Just this once, you'll understand, as it's a double celebration: my niece and Yvette. This is a salon, not a tap-room.

Fernande I can't wait to see what it is! What could a pauper like Vincent afford to buy you?

Yvette (*unwrapping it*) Well, we shall soon see . . .

The paper crackles, and from downstairs the lively sound of an upright piano playing a polka jangles into the quiet room

Raphaelle Well—well?

Yvette It's—it's bloody. It looks like . . . meat.

Rosa Meat?! He thinks we're hungry!

There is laughter but Yvette, shrieking, leaps to her feet letting the bundle fall to the floor. Her shrieks drown the piano and become hysterical

Yvette It's an ear! A human ear! Ah-ah . . .

*Immediately the hysteria spreads, the girls passing through aston-
ishment to fear and panic*

Raphaelle (*crossing herself*) Oh Jesu and Mary—he's carved
  somebody up.

Candice (*delirious and strangely elated*) Rubbish. It's his own
  ear.

Mme Tellier (*horrified and offended*) But how could he *do* such a
  thing? Maim himself? This is a respectable house. The Establishment at Arles has never been a subject for scandal.

Candice Fools. Are you too blind and giddy to appreciate the
  honour? (*She grabs Yvette's arm*) Yvette, the man's giving you
  himself. He can hardly do more!

Yvette (*shaking her off*) Oh who's romanticizing now? Drunken
  bitch. How do you know it's his? It could be anybody's, there
  could be a corpse outside!

*Yvette takes up the bundle and thrusts it into Rosa's hands, the
girl shrieking in terror and fainting back on to the box-ottoman*

Raphaelle Yes. Murder—murder!

Candice (*transported*) It must be glorious to have a man do
  such a thing for one. Only a real artist could think of such a
  sacrifice——

Yvette (*wild, annoyed*) Well *you* stay here and rhapsodize about
  it if you like. I'm going for the police.

The girls all start to scream and argue at the same time

Mme Teller (*taking charge, thundering*) NO—*no*, mesdames! I
  won't have it. Do you understand? I will see Monsieur le Juge
  —M. Vassi, have the man certified, incarcerated. I will not
  have my house abused, you hear? Yvette, Fernande, go down
  and entertain our guests, they must not be left alone; and
  Raphaelle, ask M. Vassi, privately, to join me here. (*She
  points to the parcel*) This—this object must be taken in charge,
  used as evidence.

*Yvette, Fernande, Raphaelle and Rosa go about their duties
chattering and exit*

Candice kneels and gathers up the ear and papers reverently

Candice It's an inspiration.

Mme Tellier (*beside herself, stamping her foot*) Oh shut *up*, Madame!

She turns round to storm out but is arrested by the calm voice of Candice

Candice Mme Tellier?

Mme Tellier turns

You will, I hope, allow me to stay the night? With the delay and excitement I fear I will obviously have missed my train.

Mme Tellier (*sneering*) You are altering your tune, Madame. You are persuaded to join us, as a giddy girl in some novelette, in the hopes you will be bombarded with pieces of anatomy from every artist in the town? It's monstrous and barbaric.

Candice I would indeed be tempted to stay for such a fate—but I'm afraid your sordid ménage cannot come up with such gestures very often. I would, however, like to take on the vacancy of wine-waitress, temporarily—just to keep an eye on Yvette. Only selling wine, of course, nothing more.

Mme Tellier The English, what hypocrites they are. Consider yourself hired, Madame, but don't expect excursions, suicides and *ears* every day of the week!

Mme Tellier sweeps out

Candice remains kneeling. The possibility had not occurred to her

Candice Suicide . . .? Oh, Vincent, please don't be—dead.

The Lights fade to Black-out

CURTAIN

FURNITURE AND PROPERTY LIST

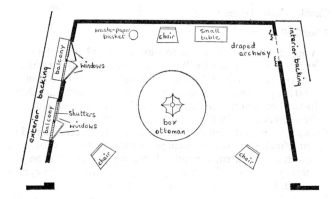

On stage: Box-ottoman

2 identical chairs. *Thrown over* DL *one*: chain of coins, bright and flounced Spanish dress

Chair

Small table

Waste-paper basket

Shutter closed to start

Off stage: Oil painting **(Yvette)**

Cake with lighted candles, flat box containing 5 pairs of garters: red, lilac, blue, golden, black with silver thread **(Fernande)**

6 plates, plate of small delicacies **(Rosa)**

6 wine glasses, bottle of wine **(Raphaelle)**

Small parcel containing "severed ear" **(Rosa)**

LIGHTING PLOT

Practical fittings required: oil lamps

Interior. The same scene throughout

To open:	Black-out	
Cue 1	At the end of the song *Bring up late afternoon sunshine effect through shutter slats*	(Page 1)
Cue 2	**Yvette** opens the shutter *Increase lighting overall*	(Page 4)
Cue 3	**Fernande:** ". . . these Spaniards!" *Start dusk effect, increasing rapidly*	(Page 16)
Cue 4	As **Rosa** lights the lamps *Practicals on, bring up interior lighting effect*	(Page 18)
Cue 5	**Candice:** ". . . please don't be—dead." *Fade to Black-out*	(Page 21)

EFFECTS PLOT

Cue 1	After **Yvette, Rosa, Fernande, Raphaelle** and **Mme Tellier** finish singing *Short pause, then bell rings persistently*	(Page 17)
Cue 2	**Mme Tellier:** "Light the lamps." *Bell stops*	(Page 18)
Cue 3	As **Yvette** unwraps the parcel *Sound of a lively polka being played on a piano downstairs*	(Page 19)

GRANDMÈRE

Waltz Moderato

Béranger/Hillman

Oh how I mi-ss my dimp – led arms, my
(Oh) how I re-gr-et my dimp – led arms, my

well – made legs and my van – ished charms.
well – made legs and my van – ished charms.

Once I was beau – ti – Ful, trav – elled
Cher- ish your beau – ty, too soon it's far married

now I'm just a grand – ma – mma! But
you'll be- come old grand-ma – mmas! And

MADE AND PRINTED IN GREAT BRITAIN BY
LATIMER TREND & COMPANY LTD PLYMOUTH

MADE IN ENGLAND